Luke Coo

WOULD YOU RATHER REVOLUTION

- By Clint Hammerstrike

About the Author

Someone with plenty of free time to write this book and enough imagination to create the name Clint Hammerstrike – seriously why wouldn't you!

What else is there to say other than you will be pleased to know this isn't my day job!

Introduction

Writing this book has been one of the most entertaining things that I have ever done (I live a very dull life – watching paint dry oooh fun)! I take great joy in pondering random scenarios and questions. If I was given a jigsaw piece every time I contemplated the questions would I rather X OR Y, I would have enough puzzle pieces to make a 10,000 piece puzzle - but as I am awful at puzzles it would stay in pieces.

I wrote this book to share with you some of the great conundrums we face in the modern age such as:

- Whether to break the record for most toilet seats broken over your head OR most straws places in your mouth?
- Suffer from Pentheraphobia (fear of your mother-in-law OR Doraphobia (fear of touching the skin or fur of an animal)?
- Work as a Festival Portaloo cleaner OR a Poop Stirrer?

The great thing about this edition is that you not only get to ponder the complexity and bask in the pure joy of each hypothetical but you get to answer by drawing your favored choice!

This Doodle Edition could have you drawing anything from you being kicked in the shins by a horse or eating a dozen penguins.

Remember all of these scenarios are for hypothetical entertainment and drawing purposes and should not be taken as a recommendation or an endorsement. You should never collect whale snot, eskimo kiss your boss or snog a bulldog. Did I really need to say that last one!?!

Helpful Guide

To aid you on this journey of self-discovery I have suggested a couple of rules to help you through.

Rule 1: You must answer. Even if you would rather do neither you MUST pick!

Rule 2: Don't rush your answer. Give yourself time to consider the sheer complexity and horror/joy of the choice!

Rule 3: Respect the opinion of those reading with you - even when they are plainly wrong!

Rule 4: Take this seriously, we are considering the meaning of life do not even consider laughing!

Rule 5: Forget rule 4. Laugh, come on its working as a Theme Park Vomit Cleaner OR odour judge!

Rule 6: Draw whatever it is that you have chosen as your favoured option. How you decide to do this is up to you. Send your best picture to clinthammerstrike@gmail.com and you could feature in a future edition! Alternatively share it online at: facebook.com/ClintHammerstrike

Let's get drawing

WOULD YOU RATHER:

Take a poo in the toilet of a fancy restaurant
and have to wipe up with your underwear
OR socks?

WOULD YOU RATHER:

Wake up naked in an art gallery OR a
supermarket?

WOULD YOU RATHER:

Live in a house with no roof OR in a house with no walls?

WOULD YOU RATHER:

Always feel like you need to pee OR poo?

WOULD YOU RATHER:

Be rich but never be able to go outside OR poor and be able to go where you like?

WOULD YOU RATHER:

Be a part of the Avengers OR X-Men?

WOULD YOU RATHER:

Have a giant unibrow OR have hair sticking
out of your nose and ears?

WOULD YOU RATHER:

Count every star in the sky or every tree in
the Amazon?

WOULD YOU RATHER:

Be hunted by Ninja's or the Mafia?

WOULD YOU RATHER:

Eat only hummus and carrots OR have to
walk with crutches for the rest of your life?

WOULD YOU RATHER:

Never be able to wear shoes OR underwear?

WOULD YOU RATHER:

Use a koala OR an owl as a towel?

WOULD YOU RATHER:

Swim the length of a swimming pool filled
with blister fluid OR runny snot?

WOULD YOU RATHER:

Have an IQ of 160 (the same as Stephen Hawking) or £160 million?

WOULD YOU RATHER:

Be able to restart your life OR continue it as is?

WOULD YOU RATHER:

Be able to talk your way out OR fight your way out of any problematic scenario?

WOULD YOU RATHER:

Lick every object you see OR be licked by everyone that see's you?

WOULD YOU RATHER:

Smell like a skunk OR look like a skunk?

WOULD YOU RATHER:

Have a head the size of an exercise ball OR a satsuma?

WOULD YOU RATHER:

Live in a tree-house OR a cave?

WOULD YOU RATHER:

Lose your sense of smell or taste?

WOULD YOU RATHER:

Be completely bald all over OR hairy all over?

WOULD YOU RATHER:

For a day be accompanied everywhere you go by a naked sumo wrestler OR spend the day dressed as a sumo wrestler?

WOULD YOU RATHER:

All the food you ever eat is free OR all the food you ever eat is calorie free?

WOULD YOU RATHER:

Fight a skinny sumo wrestler OR a lazy
ninja?

WOULD YOU RATHER:

Have no knees OR elbows?

WOULD YOU RATHER:

Have a pet unicorn OR be a unicorn?

WOULD YOU RATHER:

Accidentally share on Facebook a photo of you on the toilet OR eat a smoothie made of all the gunk in your shower plug?

WOULD YOU RATHER:

Never be able to smile OR never be able to laugh?

WOULD YOU RATHER:

Lose all the photos you have ever taken OR
all the music you have ever owned?

WOULD YOU RATHER:

Be able to pick the next leader of your
country OR invent one new law?

WOULD YOU RATHER:

Would you rather erase all trace of yourself from the internet OR have the most social media followers in the world?

WOULD YOU RATHER:

Be able to record everything you see OR
everything you hear?

WOULD YOU RATHER:

Fight Ronald McDonald, Colonel Sander OR
the Burger King?

WOULD YOU RATHER:

Hollywood made a film about your life OR
your favourite band wrote a song about you?

WOULD YOU RATHER:

Give Godzilla a colonic irrigation OR eat a
dozen penguins?

WOULD YOU RATHER:

Write great songs and not be appreciated OR
write terrible songs and be popular?

WOULD YOU RATHER:

Find your soul mate OR a suitcase of cash
that never runs out?

WOULD YOU RATHER:

Find out that your parents are aliens OR
marry your cousin?

WOULD YOU RATHER:

Break your arm surfing OR your leg skiing?

WOULD YOU RATHER:

Spend a night alone in a creepy house in the woods OR in the White House with Donald Trump?

WOULD YOU RATHER:

Be trapped in a lift with the first person you ever kissed OR your ex's mum?

WOULD YOU RATHER:

Run a marathon but on reaching the finishing line be told you have to run another 5 miles OR snog a bulldog?

WOULD YOU RATHER:

Have to walk bare foot across a room
covered in slugs OR snails?

WOULD YOU RATHER:

Rub salt OR Lime Juice into a paper cut?

WOULD YOU RATHER:

Be kicked in the shins by a horse OR in the
head by a karate instructor?

WOULD YOU RATHER:

Have to stop a nosebleed using a stranger's
pants OR their snotty tissue?

WOULD YOU RATHER:

Eskimo kiss your boss OR a pug that has just
licked it's bottom?

Working 9 to 5

WOULD YOU RATHER:

Work as a proctologist (anus doctor) OR as a crime scene cleaner?

WOULD YOU RATHER:

Work as an animal pee collector (yes that is a
real thing) OR as a manure inspector?

WOULD YOU RATHER:

Work as a theme park vomit cleaner (Thorpe Park has one) OR as an odour judge (judging how good and bad things smell)?

WOULD YOU RATHER:

Work as a medical waste disposal worker
(think limbs, needles and bandages) OR as a
mortician?

WOULD YOU RATHER:

Work as a sewer cleaner OR as a colonic irrigator?

WOULD YOU RATHER:

Work as a maggot farmer OR as a chicken sexer (they determine whether a chicken is a male or female)?

WOULD YOU RATHER:

Work as an Esthetician (includes removing puss from people's spots as they give facial treatments) OR as a slaughterhouse worker?

WOULD YOU RATHER:

Work as a whale snot collector (yes its real, and yes it's as disgusting as advertised) OR as a guano collector (fancy term for someone that collects bat and bird poop)?

WOULD YOU RATHER:

Work as a festival portaloo cleaner OR as a poop stirrer (prepare specimens for DNA testing by stirring to form a suitable solution)?

WOULD YOU RATHER:

Work as a roadkill collector (fox, badger or squirrel get your spade out) OR as an armpit sniffer (how else can deodorant companies know they are doing a good job)?

WOULD YOU RATHER:

Work as a lift pump unblocker (they work at sewerage treatment plants and have to wear full scuba gear to swim through excrement to unblock sewerage pumps) OR as a cavity searcher at a maximum security prison?

WOULD YOU RATHER:

Work as a noodler (catching Catfish by getting them to bite your arm) OR a high rise window cleaner (hope you have a head for heights)?

WOULD YOU RATHER:

Work as a rodeo clown (brought in to distract the very angry bull - good chance you are going to get a kicking) OR a clinical trial subject (let's hope you are in the placebo group)?

_____

WOULD YOU RATHER:

Work as an Alaskan crab fisherman (mortality rate 80% higher than average worker, days without showering and 48 hour straight shifts in freezing conditions) OR as a Hurricane Pilot (NASA wants to understand how hurricanes work so they have pilots who fly through them, yup real!)?

WOULD YOU RATHER:

Work as a skydiving instructor (leaping from a plane – fine, leaping from a plane with a stranger strapped to your chest who could freak out at any time – not fine) OR as a drying paint watcher (not just an expression some people are actually employed to test how long it takes for paints to dry)?

WOULD YOU RATHER:

Work as a train pusher (in Japan Oshiyas are paid to help cram people onto train carriages by shoving them in like Sardines in a tin) OR as a dog food taster (chowing down like a hound, testing new dog food products for flavour and texture)?

WOULD YOU RATHER:

Work as a snake milker (the collector of highly poisonous venom from angry snakes) OR as a naked life art model (yup, just a room full of strangers painting you in all your glory)?

WOULD YOU RATHER:

Work as a professional queuer (some rich dudes going to pay you to stand in line) OR as a golf ball diver (someone needs to collect all those balls you have hooked off the tea)?

WOULD YOU RATHER:

Work as a bed warmer (some Hotels pay people to wear sleep suits and act as hot water bottles until guests arrive) OR as a waterslide tester (as advertised, let's hope they built it right)?

WOULD YOU RATHER:

Work as a professional bridesmaid (fit in the dress – you get the job) OR as a professional mourner (cry on demand – you get the job)?

WOULD YOU RATHER:

Work as a Panda nanny (spending 365 days caring for Panda cubs) OR as a professional foreigner (some Chinese companies will pay big bucks for you to dress up and attend functions)?

WOULD YOU RATHER:

Work as a face feeler (also known as Sensory Scientists who use their hands to judge the effectiveness of lotions) OR as a professional cuddler (not sure if you are the big spoon or little spoon)?

Fear and Phobias

WOULD YOU RATHER:

Suffer from Xanthophobia (a fear of anything yellow - including the sun) OR Porphyrophobia (a fear of anything purple)?

WOULD YOU RATHER:

Suffer from Turophobia (a fear of cheese) OR
Hylophobia (a fear of trees)?

WOULD YOU RATHER:

Suffer from Omphalophobia (a fear of the navel) OR Nomophobia (a fear of being without mobile phone coverage)?

WOULD YOU RATHER:

Suffer from Ombrophobia (a fear of rain) OR Pogonophobia (a fear of beards)?

WOULD YOU RATHER:

Suffer from Chionophobia (a fear of snow)
OR Ancraophobia (a fear of wind)?

WOULD YOU RATHER:

Suffer from Dextrophobia (a fear of objects being to their right) OR Papyrophobia (a fear of paper)?

_____

WOULD YOU RATHER:

Suffer from Somniphobia (a fear of falling asleep) OR Coprastasophobia (a fear of becoming constipated)?

WOULD YOU RATHER:

Suffer from Geniophobia (a fear of chins) OR Genuphobia (a fear of knees and/or kneeling)?

WOULD YOU RATHER:

Suffer from Emetophobia (a fear of vomiting)
OR Aulophobia (a fear of flutes)?

WOULD YOU RATHER:

Suffer from Arachibutyrophobia (a fear of Peanut Butter sticking to the roof of your mouth) OR Scriptophobia (a fear of writing in public)?

WOULD YOU RATHER:

Suffer from Pentheraphobia (a fear of your mother-in-law) OR Doraphobia (a fear of touching the skin or fur of an animal)?

WOULD YOU RATHER:

Suffer from Brontophobia (a fear of thunder)
OR Tapheophobia (a fear of being buried
alive)?

WOULD YOU RATHER:

Suffer from Kathisophobia (a fear of sitting down) OR Hypengyophobia (a fear of responsibility)?

WOULD YOU RATHER:

Suffer from Lutraphobia (a fear of otters) OR
Pupaphobia (a fear of puppets)?

WOULD YOU RATHER:

Suffer from Alektorophobia (a fear of chickens) OR Linonophobia (a fear of string)?

Record Breakers

WOULD YOU RATHER:

Break the record for most toilet seats broken over your head in one minute OR most straws placed in your mouth in one minute?

WOULD YOU RATHER:

Break the record for heaviest weight lifted by
an eye socket OR the heaviest weight of bees
covering your body?

WOULD YOU RATHER:

Break the record for crushing watermelons with your thighs OR most snails on your face?

WOULD YOU RATHER:

Break the record for the most cockroaches
eaten in one minute OR most armpits and
feet sniffed?

WOULD YOU RATHER:

Break the record for hardest kick to the groin
(you're the one being kicked) OR largest
scorpion held in the mouth?

WOULD YOU RATHER:

Break the record for most maggots moved by mouth in one hour OR most clothes pegs clipped to face in one minute?

WOULD YOU RATHER:

Break the record for farthest marshmallow nose-blow OR most socks put on one foot in one minute?

WOULD YOU RATHER:

Break the record for furthest distance on a
unicycle in 24hrs OR heaviest car balanced
on head?

WOULD YOU RATHER:

Break the record for the most cow brain eaten
in 15 minutes OR the most Big Macs ever
eaten by one person

WOULD YOU RATHER:

Break the record for eating the hottest chilli pepper OR holding the most lit candles held in mouth?

WOULD YOU RATHER:

Break the record for eating the largest Pizza
OR fastest eating of a 72 ounce steak?

WOULD YOU RATHER:

Break the record for the most chicken nuggets eaten in 3 minutes OR the most grilled cheese sandwiches eaten in one minute?

WOULD YOU RATHER:

Break the record for the most M&M's eaten with chopsticks in one minute OR the most candles extinguished with a fart?

WOULD YOU RATHER:

Break the record for the largest blanket fort
OR longest human tunnel travelled by a dog
on a skateboard?

WOULD YOU RATHER:

Break the record for the most stinging nettles eaten in one minute OR most apples held in own mouth and cut with a chainsaw in one minute?

More to Come

Congratulations you have made your way through the weird and wonderful world of hypothetical questions.

I hope that you have enjoyed yourself along the way and managed to create the new Mona Lisa – or perhaps just a stickman breaking a toilet seat on their head. Is there much difference between the two?

If you have enjoyed this book or feel like you still need further hypothetical therapy, please check out the other titles in this series available in e-book and paperback on Amazon.

Also if you are feeling brave please send me through your best picture and it could feature in the next edition. Please send any picture to: **clinthammerstrike@gmail.com** or share it online at: **facebook.com/ClintHammerstrike**

More hypothetical fun can be found on:
Facebook at:
https://www.facebook.com/ClintHammerstrike
Instagram: ClintHammerstrike

Other Books

If you have enjoyed this book, please check out these other titles in the series:

Would You Rather Random: A Collection of Hypothetical Question by Clint Hammerstrike. – Containing over 300 original "would you rather" questions and unique scenarios. Available in paperback and e-book.

Would You Rather Doodle Vol.1: A Collection of Hypothetical Questions by Clint Hammerstrike. – Containing 100 unique "would you rather" questions for you to doodle your heart out to. Available in paperback and e-book.

Would You Rather Doodle Vol.2: A collection of Hypothetical Questions by Clint Hammerstrike – Containing 100 Unique "would you rather" questions for you to doodle your heart out to. Available in paperback and e-book.

Would You Rather Survival: A collection of Hypothetical Questions by Clint Hammerstrike. – Containing 150 unique "would you rather" questions based in hilarious survival situations. Available in paperback and e-book.

Would You Rather Christmas: A collection of Hypothetical Questions by Clint Hammerstrike – Containing 100 unique "would you rather" questions with a festive theme to have the whole family laughing this Christmastime. Available in paperback and e-book.

14889896R00062

Printed in Great Britain
by Amazon